Simply Exposure: A Light Bulb Moment

By

Brian Parkin

KINDLE EDITION

I0484839

****

PUBLISHED BY:

Brian Parkin at Amazon

Simply Exposure: A Light Bulb Moment

Copyright © 2015 by Brian Parkin

****

Simply Exposure: A Light Bulb Moment

Introduction

This eBook is aimed at the beginner who has recently bought a DSLR camera. Once you understand the concept of exposure, you will experience a "light bulb moment". It will last you forever.

In this eBook, I will be referring to the Nikon range of digital SLR cameras, which have their own specific terminology and menus. Please refer to your own camera manual for equivalent terms and menus.

Focus

Before I explain exposure, let me first start by saying that one of the first elements of good photography is a perfectly focussed image. There is no point in having perfect exposure if the image is out of focus. You may be able to correct the image for exposure issues in your imaging software. You will never be able to correct an unfocussed image.

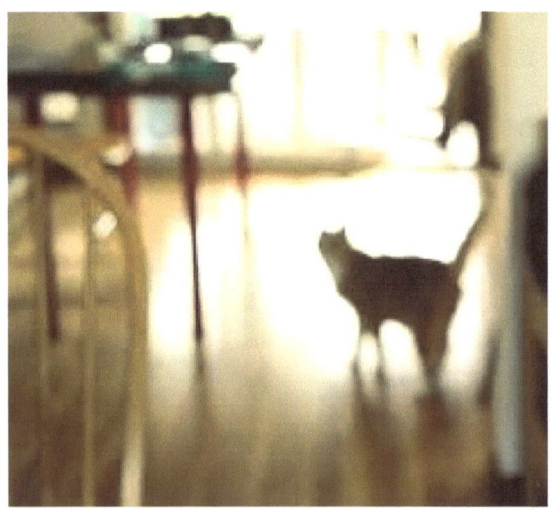

Out of focus image

Image courtesy of photomatters.org

In the good old days, pre – digital photography that is, I would shoot off a roll of film, send it off to be developed, wait several days and view my photos with great anticipation. Other photographers developed their own film and did not have to wait that long. I would often be disappointed because some part of the images would be out of focus or the highlights would be blown out, spoiling what could have been a great photo. In the photo below, you can see that the sky and parts of the lake are overexposed.

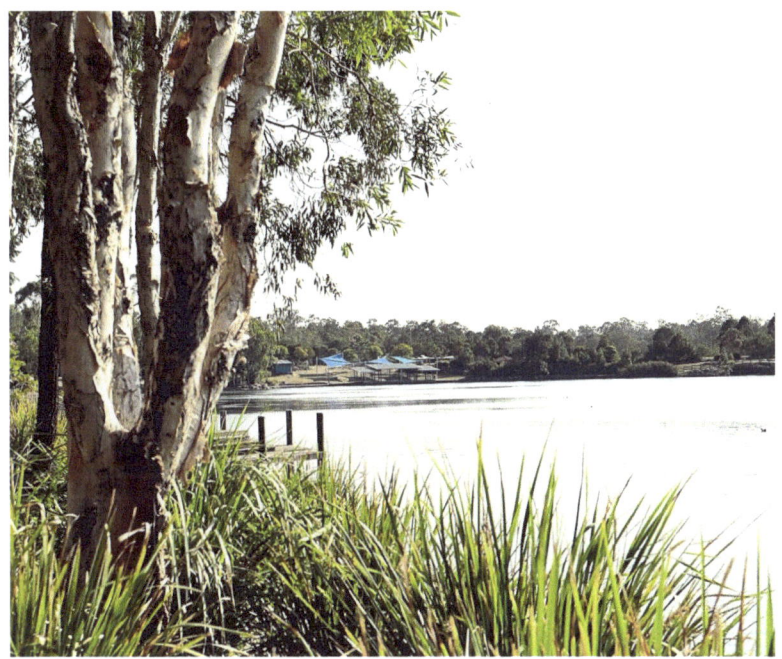

Forest Lake by Brian Parkin

Of course, now that just about all of us own a digital camera, we do not have to wait to see the images we captured. We can see the images immediately that have been captured. Some of the photos may still have blown highlights or be underexposed and we can discard them if we wish. Most of these could be saved using postproduction techniques in your favourite image processing software. However, some of us may still have to delete a significant number of images because they were taken at an incorrect focus. While it does not really matter because we can take as many shots as we want for little or no extra cost, it would be great if every shot we took was worth keeping.

I remember reading Bill Collins book "Wedding Photographer: A 45-Year Career" in which he said that when he used film, he could take 24 exposures and every one could be used in an album. Now that is confidence in his ability to take images with the correct focus and exposure for you!

Perfect Focussing Techniques

To achieve a perfect focus every time, here are a few things to consider:

Shutter speed

Very few of us can keep a camera still enough when shooting by hand, especially when the shutter speed is set at around 1/60 sec or lower. When you use a telephoto lens, the camera shake can be even more noticeable. You will need to set the shutter speed higher than what the focal length your lens is. In other words, if you are shooting with a lens with a focal length of 200 mm, your shutter speed should be at least 1/200 sec or even faster.

Stability

You can still achieve a better-focused shot while hand holding your camera if your stance is stable. The best way to hold a camera is with your elbows tucked in to your sides to provide some stability. Your feet should be slightly apart and one foot just in front of the other.

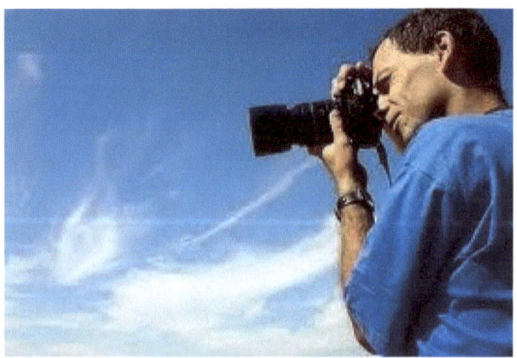

Image courtesy of Adorama.com

Your stability improves if you can brace yourself against a tree or steady your camera on a fence rail, for example. When lying down to take the shot, consider using a beanbag under your camera to provide that extra stability.

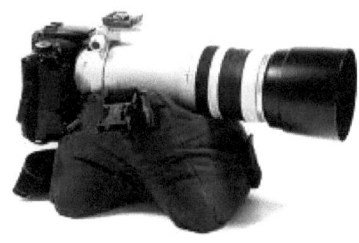

Image courtesy of news.dphotographer.com.uk

Using a tripod is ideal for many shots that require perfect focus, particularly with very slow shutter speeds. Make sure the tripod is sturdy and of good construction.

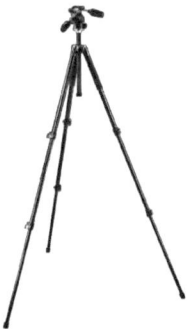

Manfrotto 290 tripod: Image courtesy of harveynorman.com.au

When shooting close ups, try using a 4 way focusing rail on the tripod, which allows you to move your camera precisely in increments, in two planes.

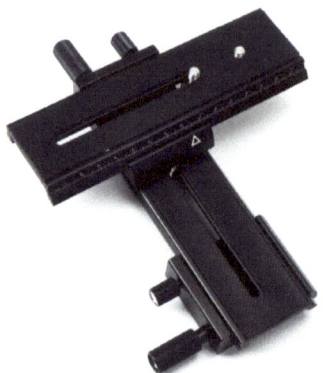

Image courtesy of pkjns.com

Shutter release

Depressing the shutter button causes image blur just from the action itself. It is recommended you use either a shutter release cable or a remote release to take the photo. These can be cheap to purchase and invaluable for your photography.

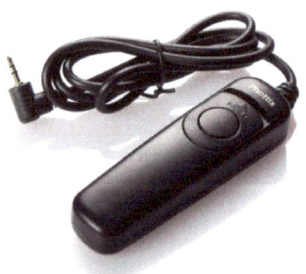

Image courtesy of cameracentreuk.com

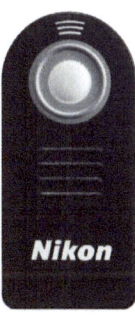

Image courtesy of Amazon.com

Auto focusing versus manual focusing

You can set focus to either manual or auto by the flick of a button, which is located either on the lens or on the camera.

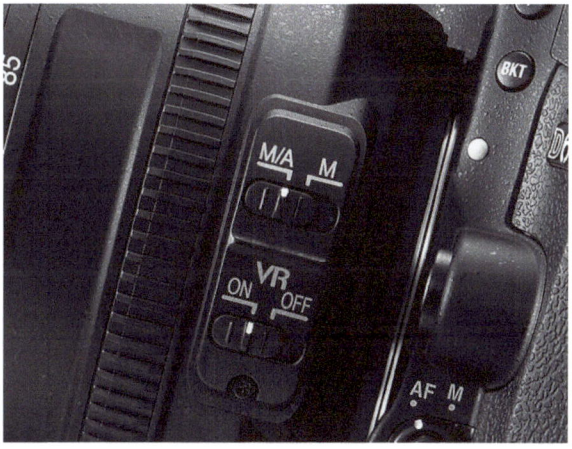

Image courtesy of digitalcameraworld.com

Auto focusing is ideal when you want to shoot quickly. Sometimes you will find that not all parts of the image are in focus, particularly when setting larger apertures for shallower depths of field.

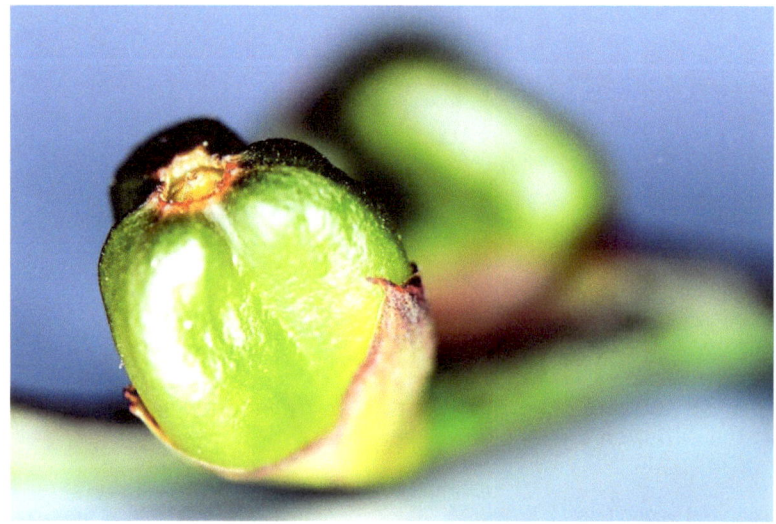

Close up of a seed by Brian Parkin

When shooting at night you could find that trying to auto focus, when there is not much light can cause the lens to hunt, that is, to fail to find the point of focus. Similarly, if you try to capture an image where there is not much contrast, the camera lens will be hunting for focus.

Manual focusing is a better alternative for these situations when used with the camera on a tripod. Use smaller apertures when trying for close ups which will bring the entire subject into focus, as opposed to just one plane of focus.

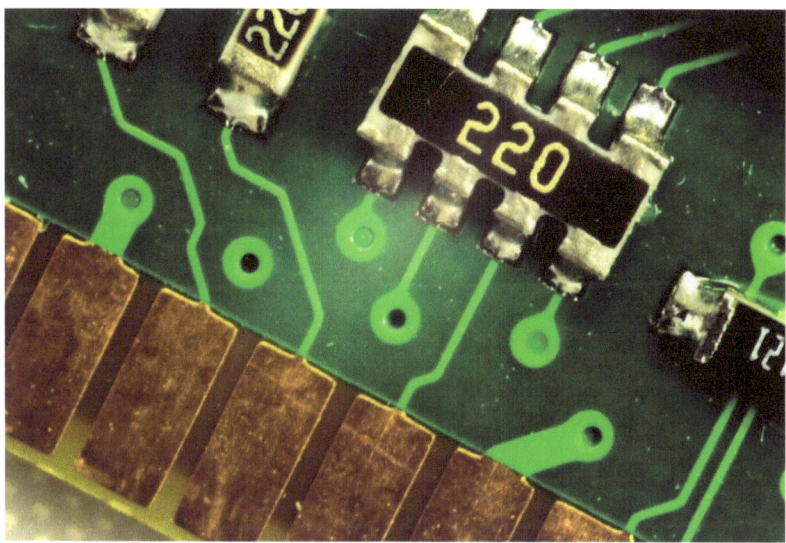

Close up of a memory chip by Brian Parkin

If you are shooting at night and there isn't much light, use a flashlight to illuminate your subject, set the focus and then take the shot without the flashlight.

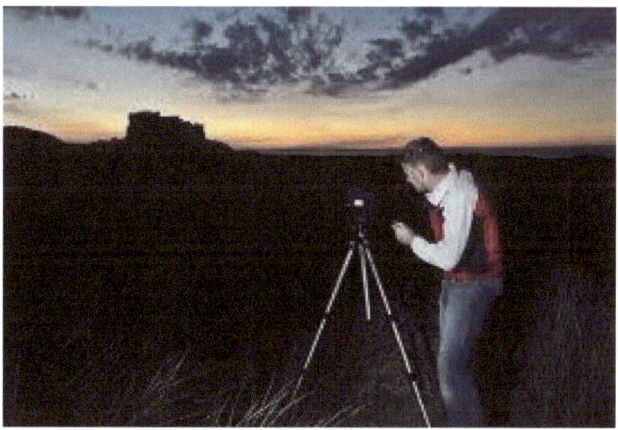

Image courtesy of digitalcameraworld.com

When shooting an object with little contrast, such as against a light coloured wall, focus on an object at the same distance from the camera, point the lens at your subject, and then take the shot. Sometimes I stick a Post-it note just to the side of my subject to obtain the correct focal point.

Live View

If your camera has a Live View option, use that combined with the magnification button to increase the size of the object you are trying to capture. This method allows you to magnify the image and apply very sharp focusing indeed. Some cameras have an LV or Live View button, other models utilise a lever on the mode wheel to activate Live View. Check your manual for further details. The particular camera below has a lever to the right of the Program Mode wheel.

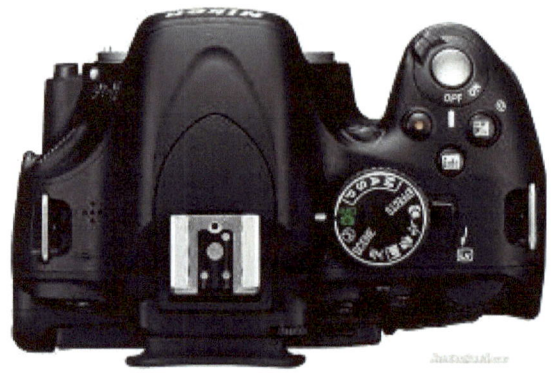

Image courtesy of kenrockwell.com

My preferred option for sharply focused shots of static objects such as landscapes and for night time shots is to have my camera on a tripod, set a small aperture, and slow shutter speed, using live view with increased magnification and by using a cable shutter release. This method works every time!

Now that you can achieve super sharp images, let us get down to the business of achieving perfect exposure every time.

Exposure

What is Exposure?

Exposure is dependent upon shutter speed, aperture size, and ISO settings. This is commonly known as the Exposure Triangle.

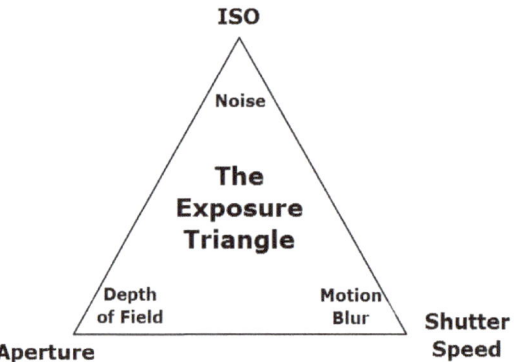

Quite simply, if one of these elements is fixed then setting a second element will alter the third element. Therefore, if we fix the ISO, and set the aperture, there will be a resulting change in the shutter speed. Similarly, fix the ISO, set the shutter speed and it changes the aperture size to achieve the perfect exposure.

Your Nikon camera has different settings for Auto, Shutter speed (S), Aperture (A) and Manual (M).

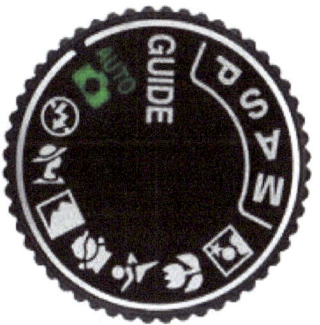

Image courtesy of Nikon.com

These terms can be labelled as something else, such as AV for aperture or TV for shutter speed, depending on the camera type.

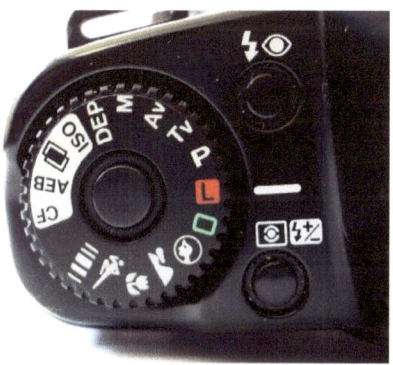

Image courtesy of canon.com

The Auto setting allows the camera to achieve near perfect exposure for the conditions at which the image is captured. You can choose Aperture mode so you can set the aperture size yourself and the camera will then choose the correct shutter speed for the best exposure. Alternatively, you can choose the Shutter speed mode, allowing the camera to set the correct aperture size for the best exposure. Manual mode allows you to be in complete control of the settings without input from the camera. The P stands for Programme Mode, allowing you to adjust the settings for say a snapshot, and is similar to Auto.

What is the perfect exposure?

Bryan Petersen, acclaimed author of his "Understanding Exposure" series, will tell you that there is not just one perfect exposure for a particular shot but there are also potentially hundreds of settings, depending what you set your camera to. There may be up to 20 aperture sizes that you could set, 30 shutter speeds and maybe 15 ISO settings or more, depending on the type of camera that you have. Each corresponding set of three components could produce the perfect exposure for the image that you are trying to capture.

How do we know if I have achieved the perfect exposure?

Thankfully, you need not worry about the hundreds of possible permutations of camera settings to achieve the perfect exposure. Your camera can calculate these for you, or at least provide assistance in doing so. It has a built in light meter, different exposure modes, a histogram of light levels, a highlights warning and an exposure grid, all of which help you to achieve the perfect exposure.

Aids to Exposure

Built-in Light meter

There is a built-in light meter in your camera, which measures the amount of reflected light from your subject that passes through your lens aperture and into the camera sensor to produce an image. The computer inside your digital SLR camera calculates the exposure based on the exposure triangle components of ISO, aperture, and shutter speed. From the computer's point of view, the perfect exposure is when there are not too many highlights so that the image is not overexposed or considered to be blown. Perfect exposure is achieved if the shadows still have sufficient detail in them. The middle ground of exposure for the camera is known as 18% grey.

Exposure Metering Modes

No scene is evenly lit. There are different areas of brightness and shadow. To achieve this middle ground of exposure, the camera has three different exposure modes, which can be set in your camera menu. You can choose spot focus mode so that the inbuilt light meter is able to measure the light in a small area of your scene; centre-weighted exposure mode so that the light meter measures a larger area in the middle of your scene, or evaluative metering which measures the average light of the whole scene.

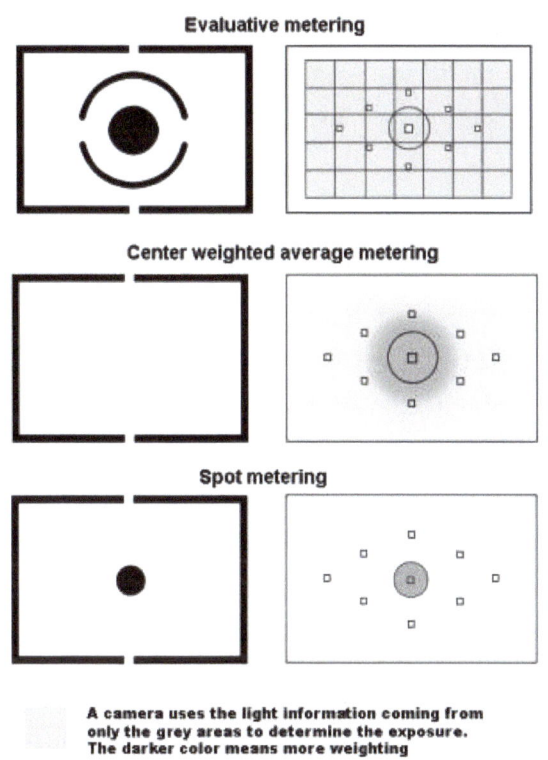

A camera uses the light information coming from
only the grey areas to determine the exposure.
The darker color means more weighting

Image courtesy of canon.com

Histogram

There are 256 discrete levels of illumination within an 8-bit image, ranging from zero, which is completely black, to 256, which is completely white. The middle ground is at level 128.

20% DISTRIBUTION GREYSCALE HISTOGRAM LAYOUT (CANON, SOME SOFTWARE, ETC.)

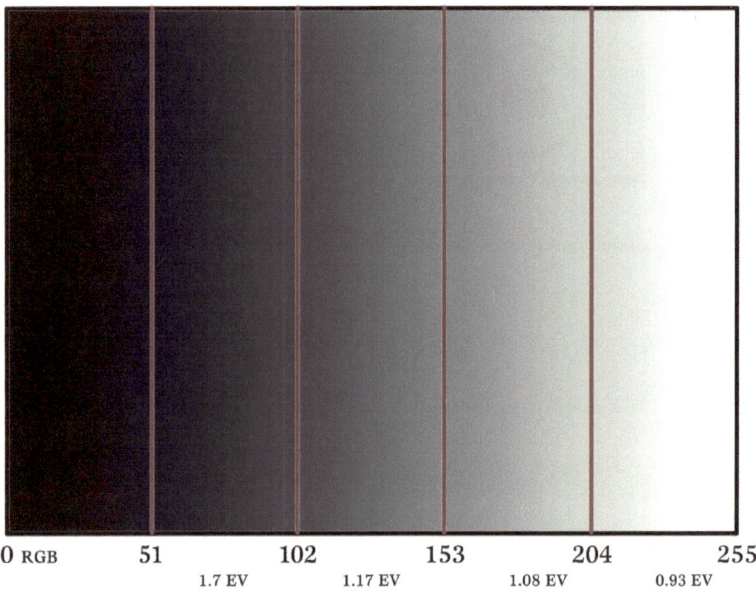

0 RGB	51	102	153	204	255
	1.7 EV	1.17 EV	1.08 EV	0.93 EV	

Image courtesy of canon.com

A histogram displaying the characteristics of perfect exposure shows a good spread across the page.

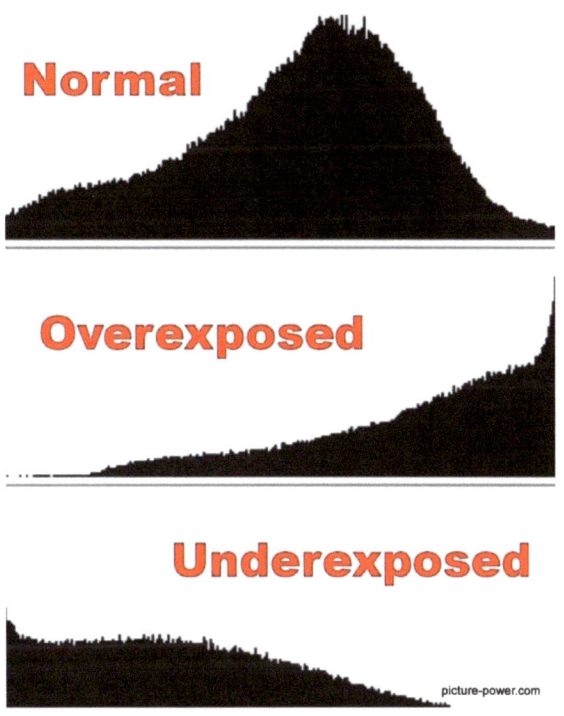

Image courtesy of picture-power.com

The height of the graph indicates the intensity of light. If there is a shift to the left in your histogram, the image is underexposed. Similarly, if there is a shift to the right, the image is overexposed. You can then change one of the parameters to shift the histogram towards the middle for perfect exposure.

Highlights Warning

Another playback display is the highlights warning,

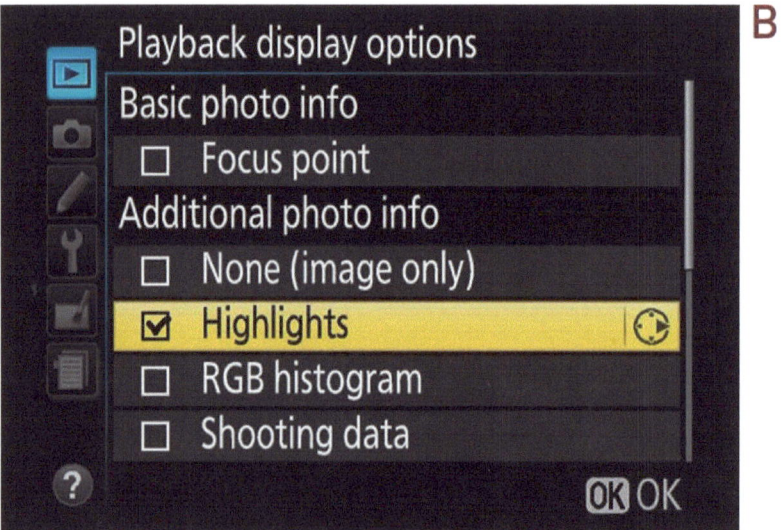

Image courtesy of Nikon.com

which can be toggled on or off and is superimposed over your playback image as flashing black or red areas, indicating blown out elements of your image.

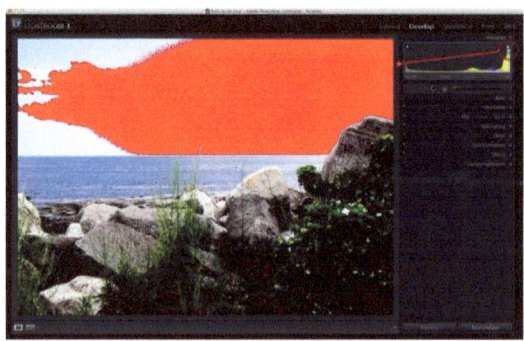

Image courtesy of lightroomsecrets.com

If your image has these red or black flashing areas, you will need either to increase the shutter speed or decrease the aperture size to allow less light reaching the camera sensor.

This is a very handy and quick way of checking for the correct exposure level.

Exposure grid

Whichever mode the camera is in, a grid appears on the display with a "–" and a "+" at either end with a 0 in the middle. (Some cameras may display the exposure increase to the left as opposed to the right.)

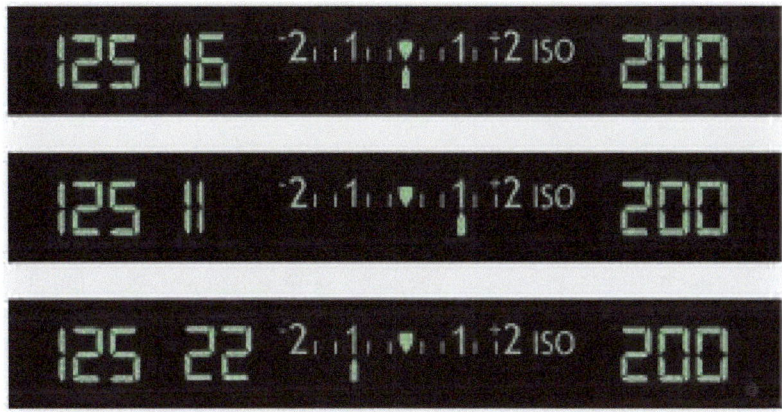

Image courtesy of digital-photography-school.com

In the top image above, the grid is indicating that the image is perfectly exposed. Increasing the aperture shifts the direction of the arrow to right in the case of the middle image. Decreasing the aperture shifts the direction of the arrow to left in the case of the bottom image. Similarly, if you were to alter the shutter speed at the same aperture and ISO setting, the arrow would shift to the left or right of the exposure grid.

Bracketing Mode

Most cameras now have a useful facility called exposure bracketing. By setting this function, the camera takes three shots of the same image. It takes one that is underexposed, one that is overexposed and one that the camera thinks is the perfect exposure.

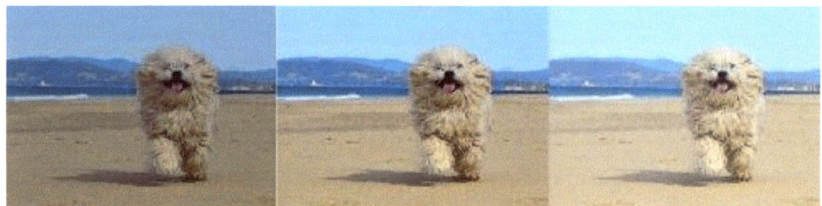

You can choose the one that you prefer.

High Dynamic Range function or HDR

HDR is similar to the bracketing mode but the camera takes only two photographs of the same scene. One of the shots is underexposed and shows detail in the shadows and the other is overexposed, showing the highlights. The camera combines the two photographs into one providing detail in both the shadows and highlights. Some dramatic and amazing shots can be produced by this method.

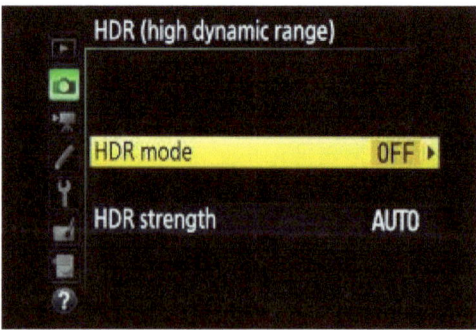

Image courtesy of photofocus.com

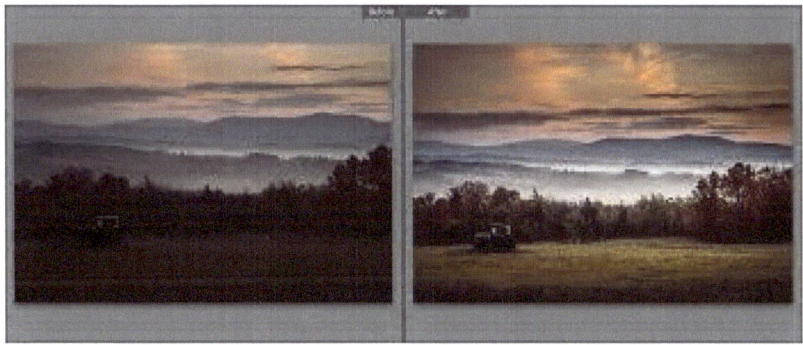

Image courtesy of lightroomkillertips.com

That concludes this short eBook on attaining the correct exposure for your images ever time. Thank you for taking the time to purchase and read my eBook.

If you have any comments, suggestions or amendments you would like me to make, please contact me to let me know. My contact details are at the end of the eBook.

Discover other titles by Brian Parkin at Amazon.com

My Other Photography Books

1. Lighting Diagrams A collection of lighting diagrams showing the setup of a camera and lighting equipment to achieve specific portrait types in a studio. This short eBook has regularly ranked #1 in Amazon Kindle in the photography lighting category.

2. The Lake at Forest Lake is a photo book featuring the wildlife at Forest Lake, Queensland. Brian is a professional photography interested in wildlife and pet photography.

My Other Non-Fiction Books

Teenage Issue Series

I wrote a series of four short eBooks covering teenage issues, which I thought would be helpful to both teenagers and their parents.

1. "Talking with Teenagers"

2. "Teens, Texting and Twitter"

3. "School Bullying Must Stop: Bullying and Cyberbullying in and out of School"

4. "Teenage Depression"

General Issues in the Pipeline

1. **"Stuttering at its Worst"**. I am contemplating writing another short eBook on stuttering. I suffered from this terrible speech impediment until I was about 21 years of age. Even to this day, in my retirement, I occasionally stutter, depending on the circumstances. In this eBook, I will share some of the ordeals that I experienced when stuttering. More importantly, I will tell you how I was able to give speeches in front of many people.

2. **"Stop Smoking and Stay Alive"**. This is another issue dear to my heart and one I have experience with for fifty years! In this eBook, I will show you how to give up, if you really want to. That is the secret. It is nothing more, nothing less.

My Thriller Novels

1. Deadly Inheritance is a murder thriller and the first novel in the Dave Pritchard series. This novel is about an ex-soldier who inherits a large sum of money from someone he befriended in Afghanistan, on the understanding that he finds any missing relatives of his friend. If he fails to find them, he inherits the lot. The missing heirs start dying like flies, leaving the ex-soldier as the only inheritor and looking like he is the culprit. He is determined to clear his name by investigating the deaths himself and find any further missing heirs.

2. The Cheng Sung Connection is the next in the Dave Pritchard series. Ian Beaufort, a freelance journalist, is on the trail of a gang of art thieves that is led by Dave Pritchard. The gang has robbed the Gallaghers of valuable artwork and when Ian prevents the thieves from collecting the money for its sale, they kidnap Joseph Gallagher's niece. Ian confronts Pritchard and is threatened if he does not back off. Inspector Joe Binks from England is called in by Gallagher to help solve the case but is in turn kidnapped by Dave Pritchard's gang. Follow the twists and turns of this novel as Pritchard, Beaufort and Binks clash in solving the mystery of the Cheng Sung connection.

3. Manifesto for Serial Killer the first in the Jessica Harper series. Learn about an independently wealthy and bored socialite who craves excitement. She decides to become the best serial killer in Australia, even the world. Realising that if she does not want to be caught, the deaths have to be completely random, i.e. no patterns that profilers can track her down with. She develops an app for her PC and mobile phone that factors in things like, location, type of victim, time of day or night, frequency of deaths or time between deaths, death weapon or cause of death, what type of person the killer is, etc. She accesses the app and it spits out all the relevant details for her next murder, which she then researches and carries it out. Jessica's kills her victims across the whole of Australia and she is determined to get to three figures before she retires as a serial killer.

Novels in the Pipeline

1. The next thriller in the Jessica Harper series will be called **"Emergency Services. Which Service Please?"** Jessica Harper switches from killing civilians and concentrates on murdering members of the Emergency Services. She uses the app to set up an accident or incident for the Emergency Services to respond to and then kills one of them. Even the police are not safe. Watch out Inspector Rob Franklin, you could be next!

2. **"Chicken or Fish, Sir?"** is the first in a series that I am currently writing. It is about a caterer, Ivy Benson and her friend, Geordie Fortune who is a food safety advisor helping her to discover who is poisoning her customers.

Connect with the Author Online

Email: mailto:brianparkin@iprimus.com.au

Twitter: @brianparkin

Blog: http://hawaygeordie.wordpress.com/